emilyfaithe.com

Music Saved My Life

Misplacing My Self-Worth and How Music Helped Me Get It Back

Emily Faithe

Copyright © 2015

Download the FREE .pdf of the discussion questions and exercises included in this book, go to:

www.emilyfaithe.com/musicsavedmylife

Why I Wrote This Book

I come from a perfectly put-together family. My parents are happily married, my siblings and I got along as well as can be expected, I went to a great private school, I had plenty of friends - so what was there to be upset about?

The truth is that I was a very lost, misunderstood teenager. I constantly felt that I did not measure up to what people expected of me. I didn't know who I was as a person. I wasn't aware that I had any particular gifts or talents to offer and share with the world. I didn't think anyone cared about me.

That led me to various poor choices in life while trying to discover myself, what I was good at, and my purpose in life. I had mistakenly believed that the sources of my worth and value were: 1. what my boyfriends thought of me, 2. my name and where I came from, and 3. my talent as a musician. But I never found any peace in these definitions of myself, and as it turns out, I am defined by something else entirely. And so are you.

This book is for all of you out there that feel like you're worthless, useless, or unwanted. This book is for all of you that don't know what you're good at, if you're worth anything, and are wondering if anyone even cares. This book is for people that want to better understand themselves, better connect with others, and find peace in life.

Hopefully by the end of this book, you will discover your purpose, your unique gifts, and your source of value as I share with you how I found my own.

Why You Should Read This Book

This book will help you learn about yourself in ways you never thought you could.

You will learn practical exercises to help heal from past hurts, and come to better know and understand yourself.

You will be joining me on my journey of self-discovery, self-expression, and finding my own source of value, but this book isn't really about me. This book is about you.

Who are you? What makes you tick? What do you have buried inside, ready to share with the world? Where does your self-worth come from? What or whom do you allow to define you?

Hopefully by the end of this book, you will have practical tactics to employ when you're struggling, you will discover your unique gifts and talents, and you will feel strong, important, and focused.

We have all come up against struggles in life, whether it be a personal insecurity, a death in the family, a divorce, an accident, or a setback in finances or achieving our goals. No matter how big or small it may seem to other people, it can be the biggest deal in the world to us and we can come to define ourselves by it.

This book is for you, in that place, so that you can break out, be empowered, and crush it in life! Join me in this partnership as you follow me on my journey and I become a part of yours.

Table of Contents

Before we begin, please rate your self-esteem right now on a scale from 1 to 10. Write it down. _____

Part I. My Three Misplaced Values

I came to think that I wasn't worth sticking around for, that I had to give more to be worth more, and that my value was in what I could offer, not in who I actually was. I want to show you how I came to think and believe these things. I don't really know why I felt them so strongly, but looking back on my teenage years I can tell you for sure that it's true.

If you feel the same, have ever believed similar lies, or know someone that does, please, keep reading.

When Music Entered My Life

I actually remember this very distinctly. There was one Christmas when I was very young that Santa had brought me a keyboard. It was probably a quarter of the size of a full-length piano, and it came with a music book to learn some basic songs - you know, songs like "Hot Cross Buns", "Mary Had A Little Lamb", and "Frère Jacques".

That Christmas afternoon, I sat myself down on the carpet and learned every single song in that book. I loved it! It was easy, relaxing, I could enter into a creative concentration, and the whole afternoon practically flew by.

My mom saw this and promptly decided that I needed to take piano lessons.

The "Child-Proofing" Process

I love to think of myself at this age - my elementary school self. When I was a child, I always had a very strong personality. When I think of myself around the ages of seven to about twelve, I use words like strong, fearless, curious, expressive, unconditionally loving, and sure of myself. I never let people walk over me or tell me what to do, but I was also very obedient to the people that had earned my respect.

If I were to define myself now as an adult, I would use very different words. I would use words like anxious, unsure, timid, lazy, concerned about what others think of me, and constantly questioning my motives, goals, and aspirations.

There's a reason people say "out of the mouths of babes." Children have an amazing ability to assess the world in a pure form and to be totally and truly themselves with no inhibition. Children see the world as it is and have no problem saying things adults wouldn't dream of voicing out loud. They experience little embarrassment, seem completely fearless, and are insatiably curious.

What happens to us as we de-child ourselves, or go through the "child-proofing" process?

Something occurred in my own life (many things, as it turns out) between my twelve-year-old self and my now twenty-six-year-old self. I think this process of "childproofing" our personalities happens to everyone as we get older, and honestly, it's a travesty.

Tornado In a Box

My mom would always call me a tornado. When I came into a room, I was loud, I was fast, I was messy, and I left in my wake a completely stunned and vibrating group of people that weren't quite sure what had just happened. I was fun, I was funny, and people loved being around me. I love that version of myself, the self I was as a child.

In adulthood, that loudness and up-frontness that I never grew out of became abrasive, an "I'm right and you're wrong" kind of attitude. The truth is that a fast pace, explosive noisiness, and a messy style just aren't as endearing when you're an adult.

If I had a dime for every time my mother said, "Emily, get out of your own little box and realize that there are other people around you!" I'd be sitting on a small fortune.

Well, as I was going into middle school and entering the more self-aware portion of my maturing process, all I began hearing were things like this:

"Why are you so selfish? Can't you see that there are other people you need to take into consideration?"

"Why are you so messy? You need to pick up after yourself."

"Why are you so loud? Take the volume down a couple notches!"

"Slow down! Why do you have to take off running everywhere?"

These are paraphrases of things my parents said to me almost every day. And here's the point I want to make very clear: these phrases – as common as they were – were certainly intermixed with many *I love yous, Great jobs,* and *We're proud of you's…* but I didn't hear those things. All I heard, in summation, was *You're not good enough, You're not what we want,* and *You can't do anything right.*

So while I never did drugs, I never drank before I was twenty-one, and was never in a gang or arrested or anything like that, I was still very unhappy. I was the squarest misfit you've ever heard of and I felt unwanted, misunderstood, and worthless.

What I want to point out is that sometimes the people that seem to have it all together — perfect families, good grades, and smiles on their faces — are actually slowly dying inside. We always assume that it's the popular kids with fancy houses and great parents that should be the happiest, most put together, and most successful people, but I know that's not true.

We all struggle. Some of us struggle immensely and some of us not as much, but depression, anxiety, and other illnesses are not picky. They host no auditions.

Loving parents, a big house, and popularity are not impenetrable shields. Many people can find themselves suffering in ways they feel they have no reason to be, and that actually makes it worse.

When I would go to sleep at night as a fifteen or sixteen-year-old, I would ask myself, "Why do you feel this way?" I had no reason to feel depressed, lonely, or worthless — but I did! But because I could never pinpoint a *reason* to feel that way, I was unable to fix it.

Misplaced Value #1 - Men

Because I was the oldest child, I was the guinea pig of the family. I think my parents were mostly reactionary when it came to figuring out what needed to be said and when. I'm sure that's the case for all parents. You make sure to say the things that were never said to you, but there will always be surprises and topics, events, and circumstances that you couldn't have predicted.

I had my first boyfriend when I was very young. I was only twelve years old, going on thirteen, and Michael was three years older than I was. I don't recall having a conversation with my parents on dating prior to that time, though it's entirely possible that we did. Either way, whatever conversation we may or may not have had definitely didn't stick.

I look now at my little sister-in-law and my cousin, who are both thirteen, and think to myself, "Now I get it. Now I understand what people saw when they looked at me with this boy." My teachers at school, my principal, and my mother all warned me that this relationship would go bad. But in my young and stubborn mind, being told it would fail only made me commit to it more. I would prove them all wrong.

Michael told me he loved me. He told me how good I was at things, how beautiful I was, and what a great voice I had. He gave me gifts, he told me that he wanted to spend the rest of his life with me. We were going to move away, buy a blue motorcycle, and live happily ever after.

As an adult I hear how naïve that sounds. It's the dream of every thirteen-year-old girl and I believed every word that came out of his mouth without question or doubt.

On our first Valentine's Day together, Michael gave me a card. I remember this like it was yesterday. On the envelope he had written *My Girl.*

I just about melted into a puddle right there on the floor. *My girl.* I was <u>his</u> girl! I belonged! This was my first real taste of what I considered self-worth: to mean something to another person, to have someone miss you when you were away, to value your gifts, your presence, and your words. Any love, admiration, and affirmation you get from your family always has implied necessity. "Oh well, you have to say that. You're family." When it comes from someone new, it means a thousand times more.

Plus, Michael was just as loud, just as fast, and just as crazy as I was, and I felt like I had found my other half.

That is, until he broke up with me.

My First Taste of Self-Doubt

Over the summer, I received a letter in the mail. It was from Michael. It started with compliments: he loved how strong I was, how I was so sure of myself, how loving and passionate I was — and then he proceeded to tell me that he didn't want to date me anymore.

But what about the blue motorcycle? What about happily ever after? What about all the promises you made me?

That's what I was thinking as I folded up the letter and put it back in its envelope. I had been lied to. I had been strung along. And it was in that moment that a veil was lifted in my mind and skepticism entered my life.

How is it that we can be so sure of something that turns out to be false in the blink of an eye? Things like that change our lives. It's happened to me many more times than this instance, but every time it floors me. You can have such strong opinions and beliefs about something that can so quickly turn out to be completely unfounded.

One hysterical example I can think of was from when I was in seventh grade. I have no idea how we got on the topic, but I very boldly stated that metal music was just noise. I said that the musicians weren't really even musicians — they just banged on instruments and called it talent.

Well, there was a boy, Jake, in that class that got really heated with me and defended bands like Metallica and Black Sabbath until he was blue in the face.

Now that I have come to love and appreciate bands like Metallica and Black Sabbath and am a better musician myself, I can clearly see how truly talented musicians like Ozzy and James Hetfield are! It may not have been my taste in seventh grade, but I was way out of line in my comments, and Jake certainly set me straight.

Sometimes these monumental moments of clarity have been for good, and other times they have been ground-shaking blasts of reality that totally took me for a loop.

When Michael broke up with me, it was the first time in my life that I grew to be distrustful. Never in my past had I assumed that someone might be lying to me, holding out a promise they couldn't keep, or shelling out a plan that they could never come through on. From this moment, reading a letter in my bedroom at thirteen years old, I learned to question people's intentions.

More than that, I began to wonder what I had done wrong, what this other girl could offer him that I couldn't, and if I could have done something differently.

My First Song

By this point I had been playing piano for four years and was starting to get more creative — not only playing what was written on the page but playing what I *felt*, imagining the stories behind the compositions, and making up my own interpretations.

After I had closed up the letter from Michael, I don't think I said anything or told anyone. I didn't cry. I didn't throw anything. I didn't even get rid of any of his stuff.

I went out into our living room with a pad of paper and a pen. I sat down and just started writing.

On a misty summer morning, I remembered the day,

You said, "I'm going" and told me to stay.

My life was perfect, but now it's torn.

Had everything a girl could want and more.

What I knew I'm not sure I know,

Am I sad, confused, not sure what to show.

I thought I knew everything about you.

I guess I was wrong.

But you never know what hell-sent silence

Could eventually turn into a heavenly song.

You told me you loved me.

You lied.

You told me you hated her.

You lied.

You sent me that letter.

I cried.

You were trying to play two games in one park.

Ended striking out and left my heart in the dark.

But I never will leave you, till death do us part.

This was my vow from the very start.

You need a friend? I'm there by your side.

You get in trouble? I'm not gonna hide.

We all deserve a second chance,

Whether we're alone or in a romance.

You left me the first time, don't do it again,

But at least through it all we've managed to be friends.

Many years later, lying alone, remembering days gone by,

You lay down beside me on a bed all our own,

And let out a working day's sigh.

"I love you" you'll whisper, putting your hand in mine.

I told you that everything would work out just fine.

The amazing thing is that this song pretty much came out just like that. I don't think I've retouched it, rewritten anything, or changed any of it. I can count on one hand the amount of times that has happened to me.

This was the first song I had ever written. In case you can't tell from the lyrics, Michael cheated on me with a girl he had explicitly told me he was not interested in. I did end up taking him back, and he cheated on me again... with the same girl. Lather, rinse, repeat.

I was young, I was stupid, and I was hopelessly in love. And I can tell you for certain that it was because of the way this situation played out that I became distrustful, insecure, and confused. Furthermore, I allowed myself to solidify those thoughts and paradigms and then carried them with me.

Misplaced Value #2 – My Name

My Father and My Dad

Around the same time that things ended with Michael, I also started to feel an ache for my father.

My father, Russell, died when I was just a year old. I never truly met him, I don't remember him, and people tell me *all the time* how much I look like him.

I began to go through a stage where my dad, Joe, whom my mom had married when I was three, was not my dad. I began to struggle with why God would allow my father to die and why I had been left behind. I felt that I didn't truly know who I was without Russell to help inform me. When people told me how much I looked like him, I felt that it was so unfair that I could be a pleasant reminder to so many people of a great man whom I would never meet. I couldn't ask my mom because she never talked about him and I thought it would be hurtful for her. But now I realize that she probably had no idea that I wanted to know. It was something that had happened so long ago for her that it probably never even crossed her mind to tell me about it. She had struggled, suffered, and moved on while I was only just beginning that process in my own life.

And the truth is that Joe raised me. He adopted my sister and me when he and my mom got married and then had my two younger siblings. I NEVER thought of Joe as my stepdad in any way or my youngest siblings as half siblings. Not once in my whole life.

But somehow I really struggled with losing my father. I wrote a lot of songs about Russell, about what I imagined his car accident was like, how I imagined my mom felt hearing the news that her husband had been killed while she was five months pregnant with my sister.

I began to see my value in being Russell's daughter. And because I didn't really know what that meant, I had a hard time working out who I was.

It was through writing songs that I started to uncover and release how I felt about him and about my relation to him. I am also willing to bet that I really freaked out my mom and my piano teacher, and I often wonder what they thought when I'd play them my songs. Here's one example:

It's been fifteen years since he passed away.

Never once have I seen his grave.

Wouldn't it be nice for him to let me know,

Just how much he loved his little girl?

The heart inside me needs to show,

All the memories I will never know.

There's something in that name,

The name I couldn't save.

My identity – taken away.

I don't remember the night he died,

But I can imagine what it must have been like.

A simple phone call to wreck our dreams.

Her whole life ripped at the seams.

She went to the hospital with her father.

No loving husband standing beside her.

She's all alone.

She brought into the world another baby girl.

The same blood runs through her veins.

He's the father of two. Only lived to see the first.

The endless emptiness still remains.

There's something in that name,

The name I couldn't save.

My identity – taken away.

I must have written that when I was fourteen years old. I so clearly felt that there was a piece of me that had been taken away, something that was mine, but that I wasn't allowed to have. Reading these lyrics now, I think I also felt that if Russell had really loved me he wouldn't have died. How ridiculous is that? But I think that's how I felt deep down. Somehow my subconscious told me that if I was worth sticking around for, he wouldn't have left.

Misplaced Value #3 - Music

About a year after Michael and I had broken up, when I was a freshman in high school, I started dating a boy named José. He was a musician like me — he had a band, he played bass, he wrote songs, and we seemed like a really great match.

I put a lot of value in my musical ability by this point, and I knew that it was something I was really good at and probably the one thing that I actually excelled in.

Being a part of a band, musical group, or choir made me feel like I was part of a whole, that I was needed and important. It was also something I was definitely better at than others, and that made me feel special, irreplaceable, and powerful.

Had I been older with a little more perspective, however, I would have seen that all José and I ever talked about was music, that we were much better friends than boyfriend and girlfriend, and that we probably should never have dated in the first place. But my value was placed in what men thought of me, and at the time, I felt that I needed to give my boyfriend whatever he wanted so that my value would increase and he couldn't leave me.

Well, that is an epic recipe for disaster. What happened because of this misplaced sense of worth is that I engaged in a highly physical relationship, one that I was deeply uncomfortable with, but that I

24

would never stop, express my discomfort in, or try to change because I was afraid that he'd leave me.

I began to create a second personality. I was one way with my family, at school, and at church, and a totally different way with my friends and boyfriend. I would play piano at church for Mass, I belonged to many musical groups at school, I was being mentored by my principal to play guitar and better piano, I got good grades, I participated in family gatherings. But I was also lying to my parents, saying I was going one place and actually going another, and would do things that I knew would get me in trouble. I was making rude jokes and talking about inappropriate subjects so that my friends wouldn't think I was a prude. With my friends, I was becoming that teenager that thinks she's just too cool for all that lame church and family stuff. I wanted to be at concerts, off on my own, hanging out with my friends that had no rules or expectations over me. Yet I also had a constant uneasiness in my heart.

As human beings, we are both a body and a soul. When the body and soul aren't getting along, stress, confusion, and uneasiness enter our lives. At this time, my body and my soul were saying, doing, and truly believing two opposing things and that was creating a lot of stress, anxiety, and discomfort in my life.

Looking back on it, I think, *Would it have been such a big deal if José and I had broken up?* No way! But my self-worth was all tangled up in José's desire for me. If he broke up with me, it would only solidify that I was worthless and unlovable.

Well, in the end I broke up with him. I became far too uncomfortable and I was getting into some trouble with my parents and my friends' parents.

But I left that relationship with a specific event burned in my memory. Because José was a musician and wrote his own music, I wanted to share with him some things that I had written. My grandparents had bought me a four-track for Christmas and so I recorded a little something to share. The recording was pretty terrible — my guitar was way out of tune and you could hear people talking in the background.

When I showed it to him, all he said was, "You should really think about tuning your guitar the next time you record."

I was absolutely crushed. The song had been one about my father, and I was trying to share that part of myself with José through this song and hopefully collaborate with him. But, instead, his comment only served to solidify my own idea that I wasn't good enough, even when it came to the one thing I really thought I was good at.

All Of My Misplaced Values Working Against Me

That next school year, after José and I had broken up, I thought I had hit the nail on the head. I had been super good friends with this boy James since we met in seventh grade.

James was also a musician and bass player who wrote his own music. He was an emotional artist like me, and really loved talking things out, asking good questions, and diving into the meaning of things.

James and I pulled together a small band with my sister Wendy and a couple of my cousins. We'd get together and get absolutely nothing done, but we had a cool name and a logo and loved to dream of the future days when we'd travel and perform.

None of that ever happened.

There came a point in our friendship, though, when James and I became a little more than friends and we talked about dating. We recognized the possibility that our friendship could be damaged if our dating relationship didn't work out… but did I mention that we were both highly emotional artists?

While José and I really only shared our love of music, James and I shared almost everything in common. You know how people say that opposites attract? I think the more appropriate version should be that opposites work! James and I were practically the same person — we shared all the same strengths. When you say that you are one half of a whole, that implies that there are traits in the other person that you are missing. The other half completes you. James and I were not like that. We were the same.

At first glance, that seems awesome! We liked all the same things. We got excited about all the same bands, books, and events. We operated the same way in thinking, processing, and reacting. How could that be a bad thing?

Here's why: while we shared all of the same strengths, we also shared many of the same weaknesses. We tended to get upset easily, to immediately go for the cold shoulder tactic, and to not know how to handle disagreements.

That led to a lot of fighting.

I remember my mom saying to me, "You know, Emily, dating is supposed to be fun."

I had forgotten that. Or maybe I never really knew it. Dating *is* supposed to be fun! And what James and I were doing was really not fun. It had started out that way, but that's not what it became.

We had become best friends. We were friends all along, but it was in dating that we accidentally made each other our whole lives. My entire life revolved around, was anchored upon, began and ended with James. My identity was in being the half that went with him. We were totally involved in each other's families, we didn't really have any other friends besides each other, and every free moment we had was spent doing something together, writing to each other, or thinking about each other.

If you're thinking, *That seems really unhealthy*, that's because it was! I had never had any close girlfriends and I really was quite a tomboy growing up. That posed a problem for me when I was dating because I didn't have the clarity and support you get from having girlfriends in your corner, and I couldn't have any other close guy friends because that would have been inappropriate when I was exclusively seeing someone.

I think James and I both hit a point where we had had enough, and during a very emotional phone call, we mutually agreed to break up.

The Truth About Depression

I felt like my best friend had died.

We had talked about the possibility that dating could ruin the friendship we had built. We had calculated the risk, but I really didn't think that it would feel the way that it did. To be honest, I didn't think we would ever break up.

Because James was really the *only* friend I was with for almost a year, when we broke up I found that I had no one to turn to. I had cut off the few girlfriends I did have, plus my siblings, my cousins, and my parents. I felt totally and completely alone. On top of that, I thought that they would all be angry that I had ignored them for so long that I felt I couldn't approach them. And on top of *that*, James had introduced me to all my favorite bands. All of my most recent songs I had written with him. After we broke up, everything music-related reminded me of him and I found that I couldn't play, write, or listen to music anymore.

If you were to go through my journals and manuscripts, you would find a very thorough chronicle of almost my whole life. You would also notice a giant gap in the story.

This is that gap.

I had no boyfriend and I didn't have my music, and because my identity rested in those things, I didn't know who I was without them.

I'd wake up in the morning and dread going to school. I'd sit through class and be constantly aware of James' presence. I avoided him every moment I could. I started hanging out with my cousin and his friends in the grade below me just so I could breathe a little. I'd get home and dread doing homework. I'd sit down to dinner and feel like puking. I'd get in bed and dread going to sleep. All of that eventually turned into a total numbness. I just didn't *want* to do anything. I didn't want to get up and I didn't want to go to sleep. I had no interest anymore in my favorite things and I didn't want to talk to anyone.

I had always thought that depression was a choice. I couldn't understand why depressed people couldn't just pull themselves up by the bootstraps, suck it up, and get on with life. But the truth is that when you are deep down at the bottom of a proverbial well, Lassie isn't coming to get you out. You're so far down that you can't even see the light from the opening. There's no paths to walk down and nobody's hand to grab. You're just sitting there by yourself, waiting.

My Lassie

At the end of each year, the studio where I used to take piano lessons holds a recital of sorts. It's way cooler than a normal recital, though. Instead of a boring, stuffy parade of single performances, all of the teachers bring their students together to form small bands and cover popular songs.

That year, after James and I had broken up, my piano teacher convinced me to play one of my original pieces. There was a song that I had written about James and that was the one we decided I would play.

Snuggled up in bed with the memories of yesterday,

Wishing away all the heartache that's bound to come.

`Cause we're having way too much fun in these sands.

Nothing this good lasts forever, so I'll take what I can.

Fly away over the rainbow.

Touch the skies of never never land.

I love you to the moon and back.

I gotta tell you, gosh I hope this lasts.

Every second I spend lost in your eyes,

I'll never find my way back. I'm hypnotized.

What did I tell you about keeping your hand in mine.

I'll helplessly follow, if you lead me, to the end of time.

Waiting backstage before I performed it, I met a boy named Matt. Want to know the best thing about him? He didn't know me. He didn't know I was depressed. He didn't know I was struggling.

He started asking me questions about myself, where I was from, what I played — all that normal getting-to-know-you stuff. It was the first time in a long time that I felt drawn out of myself, like someone had reached down into that well and extended a hand. That is the beauty of community. There is an instant drawing out that happens when you share your life with someone else, even in the most insignificant ways.

I never really told Matt this, but he saved me that day. Because of how much I had grown to value men's opinion of me, I think only a man could have helped me.

I played my song with strength and a sense of creative power that I hadn't experienced in a very long time. Afterwards, Matt highly complimented me. He couldn't believe that I had written it. He was amazed by my playing. Within those compliments I started to replace some musical memories. Music slowly started to become mine again and I began to fall back in love with playing and writing.

That following year, I wrote more songs than I have ever written. I almost stopped learning new songs altogether and would bring my piano teacher a new piece each week. She would help me work through it, add accompaniment, and work on better lyrics. She would often pull the studio owner into our practice room so I could play it for him as well.

I was starting to feel like myself again. Matt and I became really good friends and he helped me talk about my feelings and frustrations. He asked really good questions, reaffirmed my talents, and pointed out some gifts I didn't even know I had.

But as you can see, I still very much placed my value in Matt's opinions and my giftedness as a musician. I can honestly say that I am still to this day working on not placing my value in what other people think of my ideas, talents, or appearance.

Discussion Questions

Answer these questions in your own journal during some quiet time, or better yet, discuss them with a group of peers. Just make sure you write them down so that you can come back to them in the future.

Who Are You?

1. How would you describe yourself as a child?

2. How would you describe yourself now?

3. Is there anything different about yourself now compared with who you were as a child that jumps out at you?

4. What were your favorite things to do in the past?

5. What are you favorite things to do now?

6. What are your deepest values, the things you will not compromise no matter what?

7. What causes do you strongly believe in or connect with?

Where are You Currently Placing Your Value?

1. When you are having a bad day, whom or what do you turn to first?

2. If you have a question, whom or what do you seek for an answer?

3. If you want to know if something looks good on you, whose opinion matters most?

4. If you were to ask, "Am I doing a good job?" whose opinion would matter most?

5. If you are having a personal problem, whom do you seek to help you work it out?

6. Recap: Who is the person or thing that appears most in your answers? Is this an appropriate person or thing for you to derive your value from?

Rank the following 10 words in order of importance:

Achievement   ____

Challenge   ____

Beauty   ____

Comfort   ____

Education   ____

Health   ____

Intimacy   ____

Spirituality   ____

Passion   ____

Adventure   ____

Part 2. Re-Defining My Value

The Man That Changed It All

When James and I broke up, I swore off boys.

I made a deal with God. It was a silly thing, but I have found that God honors even our most ridiculous prayers if they will work towards our good.

No one had ever given me a rose and I knew that people often prayed for roses as signs for their prayers. So I told God that the first man to give me a rose would be the man I was meant to marry. I also promised myself that I wouldn't date until I was in college.

Each school year, our high school put on a play production. Our drama program was mandatory for all students, so I was obviously in it. That year we did three one-act plays. I was the co-lead role with Justin, who was a boy in my cousin's class that I had been getting to know, in *The Devil and Daniel Webster*. Justin played Jabez Stone and I was his wife, Mary Stone. We got to play a scene at our wedding, cut our wedding cake, fall into a terrible trap when Jabez sells his soul, and then be reunited at the end with a big sloppy kiss and everything. The cast was mostly made up of the boys in my cousin's class that I had been hanging out with.

It is a very interesting thing when you spend time with people that you have known, but not really *known*. I had viewed my cousin and his group of guy friends as a single unit, with one personality, and one agenda. But doing this play with them, I began to discover each of their unique personalities and idiosyncrasies.

After the play was said and done, a friend of mine had said that Justin liked me. Well, I had made a promise to myself. No dating. On top of that, our English teacher (who was also our play director) recounted a story to me about a boy she knew in college that she was in a play with. He had come to like her a lot through the process of their time together, but it turned out that he had really fallen in love with her character and not her.

So what did I do? I called Justin up. Told him I wasn't interested. Told him I wasn't ready to date. No thank you.

Keep in mind that Justin had never even said anything to me. It's hysterical to look back on this conversation and realize how crazy I must have sounded, how out of the blue that phone call must have been.

Only later I would find out that, at the time I had called, he was actually out on a bike ride trying to figure out if he should pursue me or not. When I called and told him that I wanted nothing to do with him, it was in that moment that he decided he was going to marry me. Crazy, right?

Well, he really won me over. Since I had become close with him and his friends, we spent a lot of time together that summer, and on August 14, 2006, Justin and I started dating.

Justin is independent, strong, sure of himself, funny, really smart, and simultaneously careful and carefree. It was in him that I was reminded of all the things I used to be as a kid. But his independence also threw me for a loop. He didn't *need* me. But what became clear is that even though he didn't need me, he *wanted* me.

Then came September 14th, our one-month anniversary. I was standing in the hallway at school in front of my locker and I saw Justin walking towards me with a *rose* in his hand. I froze. He gave me a hug, wished me a happy anniversary, and handed me the rose.

I thought, *What are you doing to me, God?* I chose in that moment to forget the deal I had made. There was no way that a few short months after I had made this deal with God that He was already giving me this sign. I wasn't going to be ready to get married for years! So I ignored it.

N.E.T. Ministries

Justin and I dated that whole year, and when I graduated, I decided that I was going to join N.E.T. Ministries.

N.E.T. is a Catholic organization that recruits volunteers, ages 18-28, to go out and preach the gospel all over the country. All of the missionaries travel the country in vans and put on retreats and workshops for middle school and high school students.

I went out to Ohio to interview for a spot, was accepted, and was also invited to go a week early for musician's training.

Leaving home was a very emotional thing for me. I had never been away from home and I knew that, for the first month I was in Minnesota, I wasn't allowed to have my cell phone on me. I was really *leaving*. All of my other siblings, as they graduated high school and chose their next steps, were all a short car or bus ride away. I left New Hampshire for Minnesota. You can't really even drive that in a whole day. Nobody could simply come pick me up if I got sick or lonely.

As I said goodbye to Justin and I very tentatively asked what was going to happen, he said, "What do you mean?" Well what I meant was, *Were we breaking up?* I didn't expect him to wait around for me. He still had a year of high school left, and I wasn't going to be very available to him. I was terrified of his answer.

As it turns out, he had never even considered breaking up. He said, "Don't be crazy. Go have fun. I'll be here when you get back."

"Really?"

"Of course!"

His security and independence allowed him to let me go and have confidence that I would return to him. I did not yet have such confidence. I could see how serious and how sure he was when we had this conversation. I was 100% certain that he would wait for me, but what I struggled with was whether or not I was worth the wait.

I cried going through security, I cried on the plane, I cried on the bus ride to the N.E.T. Center, and I'm pretty sure I didn't stop crying for about a week being there.

I was so nervous to meet one hundred strangers, I didn't know what was going to be expected of me and I didn't know where I was going to be serving — it was all very overwhelming.

On top of that, as I entered the big meeting room on Day 1 of music training, all the other musicians were lining up their guitars against the wall. Then our instructor informed us that we would not be touching our instruments for the first few days.

What?

Inside I was utterly outraged. What the heck was this guy talking about? Didn't we come to *play music*? I was so confused, frustrated, and sad. Playing was the one thing I knew would calm me down and help me acclimate to this new adventure.

Well, as it would turn out, this one mandate is what has changed the course of my whole life. The reason we were not allowed to touch our guitars was because we were learning where to appropriately place our worth, something I had struggled with my whole adolescence.

Re-Defining Myself

At music training — away from my phone, away from my family, and away from Justin — I was taught that I was not a musician, I was not a girlfriend, I was not a daughter. My former identities were effectively replaced with a strong and immovable identity in Christ. I was a daughter of God first and foremost and for all time. Whatever I did from that point forward would be driven by the knowledge and power that comes from having an inheritance from my Heavenly Father as an adopted child.

Playing music was then not about proving my worth, or having a "thing," or being better at something than everyone else.

Playing music became an intimate expression of prayer, thanksgiving, and personality. A musician, in essence, is someone that praises. For Christians, that makes all of us that praise God musicians in one way or another. In my old way of thinking, that fact would have been detrimental, because I thought being a better musician than other people made me special. But the truth is that we are special because we are God's. Period.

Sisterhood

I never had girlfriends growing up. Girls were mean, untrustworthy, and just constant drama. Boys were so much simpler, easier, and more fun to be friends with.

But a major gift that serving with N.E.T. afforded me was the knowledge of the incredible importance of sisterhood. Each week, my four team sisters and I would have a sisterhood outing. We would go out and get ice cream or do a scavenger hunt or create something artistic or dance or whatever! They became some of my very best friends, and still are to this day. I had never met a group of women that so genuinely had my best interests at heart, wanted to see me succeed, and really cared about what was going on with me. I had never had a loving female perspective from peers in my life. That changed something deep inside me. It connected me with a community that truly loved me, allowed me to share things and ask questions that I never could have shared with or asked a guy, and my unique femininity was affirmed.

For example, one day, my team sister Angelle gave me a mason jar that had a paper label on it that said *Knowledgeable Beauty*. Inside the jar she had cut out slips of paper with quotes on them from famous people, Scripture verses, and poems that illustrated how knowledge can be beautiful. She always told me she admired my insatiable desire to learn new things and that mason jar was her way of never letting me forget it. It was a physical reminder and affirmation that my nerdiness was beautiful.

Then, when we were all at our team brother Dan's house for Thanksgiving, a friend from home called me and we talked for a bit. In the car with this friend was the new girl in their class.

"Emily, you're on speaker. Say hi to Joanna," my friend said.

"Hey Joanna!" I said.

All I heard was giggling.

"Hello?"

"We're here, sorry!" my friend said louder than necessary.

"Hey," said a voice I didn't recognize. *Must be Joanna.*

The conversation continued to be just as awkward, and that was the first time I spoke to my very best friend in the whole world.

Joanna (my first, best girl friend) and I always joke that we can't really remember the first time we truly met. It just seems like we have always been a part of each other's lives, and, in a sense, we have been.

During N.E.T. training, I slept on a bottom bunk. My team leader had chosen specific Scripture verses for each person in our group and mine was taped to the underside of the top bunk. As I got in bed that night, I read this:

"For I know the plans I have for you, says the Lord. They are plans for good and not for disaster, to give you a future and a hope." (Jeremiah 29:11)

The Lord knew that I would need to join N.E.T. He knew I would need Joanna. He knew that Justin would be a great partner for me. Knowing all of that, God orchestrated each piece so that N.E.T. Ministries would come across my path many times during high school, that Justin's parents and mine would send us both to the same school, and that Joanna's family would move her to New Hampshire from Maryland. Each piece was moved perfectly into place so that all of these blessings could be made possible.

Being able to see these things in my past, I am hopeful that the future will be the same; unfortunately, we can't see the pieces moving until they are in place.

My Worth

I learned that my worth and my importance come directly from God's love for me. We are *adopted* sons and daughters of God.

Let me explain what a hugely important lesson this was for me. Joe, my dad, had adopted me when I was three, when he married my mom. He didn't *have* to adopt me. I could have kept my original last name with my sister and had a stepfather. In my middle adolescent years I probably would have rather had that! But consider how much more beautiful adoption is: my dad *wanted* me. He *chose* me. He looked at me and said, *I am proud to call you my own. I want you as my daughter. I want to show you off to all of my friends and introduce you as my kid, my offspring, one who shares my name and my legacy.* That's what my dad did for me.

The reality? That's what my heavenly Father did for me too. He looked at His creation, us, and said, *This is good. These are my people and I am their God. I want to bless them abundantly and intimately share myself with them. I want them to have an inheritance of my Kingdom.* And so He adopted us.

Yet in my immaturity or ignorance or blindness I failed to see both of those realities. I was especially loved and chosen two times over and I couldn't see it!

We need to move past the mindset that people's worth is set by where they come from or the power from their family name. And we need to stop believing that ourselves. None of that matters.

Michael had made me a lot of promises that he was unable to keep. The great thing about God is that He is a God who keeps His promises with no exceptions. St. Paul talks about the biggest promise of all in his letter to the Romans:

"For the wages of sin is death, but the gift of God is eternal life in Christ Jesus our Lord." (Romans 6:23)

If we were given what we deserved, we would all be totally screwed. Whether we like to think about it or not, we are all sinners and St. Paul says that we deserve eternal death. But God doesn't give us what we deserve. He gives us what He wants us to have because He cherishes our very selves and wants to spend eternity with us. He has promised His children eternal life.

Our Eternal Inheritance

So how do we opt in to receive this divine inheritance?

Baptism.

If you have not yet been Baptized, take some time to seek it out, learn about it, and consider accepting this FREE gift from God — salvation! Don't feel worthy? That's okay. None of us are. But if you want a piece of God's infinite and divine inheritance as an adopted child of God, you have to join the family.

The doors are open. Come on in!

Bullseye

After I started to settle into this idea of having my identity in Christ, all the other confusing, floating, restless pieces started to take their appropriate places.

Every self-definition started to have its place in God, and the great thing about that is that God doesn't change. He is the only immutable being, and that makes Him a really great target. When we aim for moving targets, we will constantly be disappointed when we arrive and find out that the goal has changed course. When we aim for God, we will always know where we are going, where we have come from, and how to fit everything else in.

My Gifts

It was through this slow process of realization that I came to accept my true gifts. I had constantly put my value in moving, changing, fickle sources and so I was never able to solidly claim any of my unique gifts. I had always known that I loved music and I enjoyed playing piano and guitar, but no one had definitively and authoritatively declared that it was a gift I had.

The year that I served with N.E.T. Ministries, I was chosen as Music Leader for my team. There were about thirty of us that went to music training and only twelve that were prayerfully chosen to lead their teams. I was one of them. That was a *huge* affirmation for me.

My team and I also participated in a charism discerning retreat. A charism is a special manifestation of the Holy Spirit that we are given in Baptism in order to build up the Church. By reflecting on our personal experiences, objective results, and feedback from other people, we were all able to discern our top few charisms or gifts.

My top two were writing and music. *These* were the definitive answers to what I really had always known but never really believed. My team members reinforced that they saw those gifts in me, and that further solidified my belief.

I discovered through this retreat that affirmation of our gifts is vitally important to discerning what our gifts are, but the value, worth, and power of those gifts come directly from God. That was a subtle yet powerful shift in my understanding. When people compliment my voice or my playing I always just say thank you. If people ask me more about it, I always say that it is a gift and that I am glad they have been blessed by it. I am proud of the practice I have put into my craft, but I was born with this voice and this ability to play. No one but God deserves the credit for that.

Knowing what our gifts are gives us purpose in life. We don't become depressed or bored because we don't have enough to do. We become unhappy and de-motivated when we lose our sense of purpose. Once you know what your gifts are, you can start using them to fulfill your unique purpose, and that will bring your life meaning and fulfillment.

Music has always been the obvious gift in my life. I have had to work harder at my other gifts and talents. There is no question that music is the medium that God uses to speak to others through me.

My purpose is to use music to bless and inspire others, to share God's message for His people, and to connect with people on an intimate level that only music can accomplish.

What are your gifts? What is your purpose?

If you feel like you don't have any gifts worth sharing, think about this: you are like a snowflake — created completely unlike any other human being. God *has* given you gifts to share with the world. Ignoring or denying that you have those gifts is saying that God made a mistake (and He doesn't make mistakes) or that He gave you something worthless, and neither of those statements are true.

There is a girl that I know who is an incredible artist, but every time I would compliment her work she would say, "Oh no, it's really not that good." Except that it is! It's amazing! This is *false* humility, when you refuse to recognize and gratefully accept your giftedness.

It is through humble recognition of our own gifts that we can change the world.

My Dignity

I found that I needed to take the power I had given men to define my value and give it back to God.

Justin wrote to me every day the year that I was with N.E.T. He wanted to share in that journey with me. He wanted to grow alongside me. He wanted to support me. He was committed. He was *in*.

Four other people that served that year with me had left a boyfriend or girlfriend at home. Justin and I were the only ones still dating by the end of the year.

It's really difficult to grow so fast and to be doing something so radical and be able to stay in a long-distance relationship. When two people rely solely on each other, the relationship can't stand if one person is moving in a different direction or is growing at a different pace.

I left home and was beginning to find out who I was on my own. Justin, very gracefully, stood by my side and assisted in my growth as he mentally and spiritually accompanied me in his own growth.

I honestly believe that the only reason Justin and I stayed together was because of his willingness to sacrifice parts of a normal relationship. I saw him for a short two weeks that year while I was home for Christmas. He never complained. He never wished things could be different. He stayed up late so we could talk for five minutes. He faithfully wrote to me about everything that was happening at home, and I would return his letters with everything about my team, what we were doing, and what I was learning.

His mother will tell you how much he missed me. She says he walked around the house like a lost puppy, but he never let me know that. He never would! He made sure that I knew he was okay and that it was okay that I was gone. He reiterated that I was doing a great thing and that he loved me.

His dedication and sacrifice are why I was able to grow exponentially as an individual and we were still able to grow together through that time apart.

Discussion Questions

Who Are You At Your Best?

1. What makes you smile (activities, people, events, hobbies, projects, etc.)?

2. What makes you feel great about yourself?

3. Who inspires you most (family member, friend, author, artist, leader, etc.)?

4. Which qualities in this person inspire you? Why?

5. What would you regret not fully doing, being, or having in your life?

What Are Your Gifts?

1. What activities make you lose track of time?

2. What are you naturally good at (skills, abilities, gifts, etc.)?

3. What are you most often complimented on?

4. If you had to teach a subject, what would it be?

5. If you could get a message across to a large group of people, who would those people be? What would your message be? How would you communicate it?

Discovering Your Primary Gifts

1. Is there a word or phrase that you used to answer more than 3 questions?

2. Is there a word, phrase, or image that gave you an immediate experience of a lightbulb going on?

3. Is there a word, phrase, or image that encourages, strengthens, and uplifts you?

4. When mentally reflecting on the exercises you have just completed, what is the first word, phrase, or image that pops into mind?

Given the talents, passions, and values you've discovered, how do you see yourself using them to serve, help, and contribute to others?

Part 3. Lessons

Communication

One of the *most* important lessons Justin has taught me is to keep a constant and open line of communication. We started out our relationship with that mentality and we have never wavered in it. We talk about everything, even if it seems insignificant.

We constantly ask each other what's up when something feels off. When we were dating, we talked about getting married. We talked about our plans and dreams. He taught me to become independent and solid in my own foundation apart from him and was never thrown off when it seemed like maybe we weren't on the same page.

I remember this one time that we were in the city for an annual fireworks display. We were sitting on the pavement near the car and I asked him, if he could, would he marry me tomorrow. He said yes, without hesitation. I didn't expect him to say that. He was so sure! So he asked me back. I said no. I wasn't sure. I was still so scared that he might leave at any point and everything that I dared to hope for would be ripped from me and I'd have to start over again.

He looked at me and told me that he wasn't going anywhere. He had made up his mind. He asked if he had ever given me a reason to mistrust him or to think that he wasn't dedicated to our relationship. Of course he hadn't.

It was through these tough conversations and truthful answers that I was able to start healing, see the world for truly how it was, and to assess reality well. We so often are unable to see ourselves the way that others see us and we begin to believe lies that could be immediately dispelled if we would just share those thoughts with others.

I began to truly trust Justin. I came to a place where I knew he wasn't going anywhere and I could let myself wholly believe that we would get married. And on July 14, 2012, we did.

The biggest problem in my teenage years was that I never talked to my parents about how I felt. I couldn't. My mom actually developed a system with me where if I couldn't talk to her about something, I would write her a letter and leave it on her pillow. That way she could read it while I wasn't around and then she could initiate the conversation without me needing to express whatever was hard for me verbally.

I used songwriting like the Pensieve Dumbledore uses in the Harry Potter series to collect my pains and memories. It felt better not to have those things bottled up inside, but I also never really shared them with anyone. Every time I would play a song for someone, I secretly hoped that they would decode the deeper meaning in my lyrics and come to understand how much I was hurting. I just couldn't bring myself to share how I was feeling in a blatant and honest way.

I'm sure that in large part I *felt* unwanted, unloved, and worthless as a teenager because I didn't know how to express to others that I needed help.

When I was teenager, I had not yet grown outside of myself enough to accurately assess the world around me. When my mom would constantly tell me I needed to get outside of my own bubble, she was right! But I wasn't at an age where I was able to do that yet. I distinctly remember a day during the summer I was twenty-two: I had the immediate recognition that I was thinking clearly. I no longer felt like I had this fog in my brain when I tried to decide something emotional or close to my heart. I could hear something and better recognize whether it was true or not. I could listen to someone correct me and not feel personally attacked.

I attribute this mainly to the natural decrease in hormones as I got older. This natural course of life leads us to a place of better clarity, where we can see more of the world at once, become more empathic, and assess ourselves in a more detached way.

Love Languages

In case you are not familiar with "The Five Love Languages" by Gary D. Chapman, they are:

- Physical Touch

- Acts of Service

- Words of Affirmation

- Quality Time

- Gift Giving

We all love in each of these ways, but each of us has a top one or two that make us feel the most loved. Mine is primarily physical touch.

When Justin and I were dating, we'd be sitting on the couch and he would sit on one end and I would be sitting on the other and I would get the immediate feeling that he was angry with me. When I'd ask, he'd say that he wasn't angry, but I didn't believe him. When we would sit far apart and he wasn't holding my hand, not only did I feel unloved, I felt rejected.

I just thought that everyone loved the same way that I did, but we eventually both took the Five Love Languages Test and found out that Justin's primary love language is acts of service.

If he had carried all of my things in from the car, set up the TV, and helped me do my schoolwork, he felt that he was loving me well, even though I didn't feel particular doted upon. This worked the same in reverse. If I was sitting close to Justin, hugging him, or holding his hand, I felt that I was communicating love very clearly, even though he didn't feel particularly paid attention to or taken care of.

Early on in our marriage, Justin and I struggled with this. If clothes were left on the floor, if dirty dishes were left in the sink, or if dinner wasn't ready as soon as he got home, he felt rejected and forgotten by me.

Once we worked out that we loved *differently*, we were better able to love each other. I would purposefully make him lunch, get him blankets if he was cold, or anything else that he asked for as a means of service, and he would actively sit closer to me, hold my hand, and give me hugs.

We all have an innate desire to love and be loved. Love and partnership lie at the very heart of what it means to be human. A lot of the reason we often feel unloved by those around us, however, is because we are not being loved in our primary language.

My primary love language makes me feel connected to others simply by being physically close to them, but I always struggled with spiritual and emotional vulnerability. I allowed my lyrics and music to house the emotions and difficult thoughts that I was uncomfortable sharing with others. I wouldn't allow anyone to give me feedback or enter into the true source of my hurt with me. I wouldn't let anyone down into my well.

The Lie of Loneliness

That is one of the most dangerous things that I could have done. Separation and the feeling of loneliness can lead to a lot of these emotional deficiencies. When we believe that we are misunderstood, odd, different, we start to believe that no one else will understand what we are experiencing, so we don't share.

However, when we share ourselves with others there is a light that is cast into that dark place that we have been stuck in and we are able to see more clearly. This is what Matt was able to do for me. By asking me simple questions about myself, he drew me out of my own head so that I could share this small part of life with him. In that shared space, it's like he stepped over the crest of my well and shone a flashlight down into the depths.

Even though he had not shared my experience, just opening up to him a little bit was the difference between wallowing in despair and taking my first step out of that deep, dark emotional well.

Living in Community

There was a study done on stress and community that I came across in a TED talk by Kelly McGonigal called *How to Make Stress Your Friend*. The study followed 1,000 US adults ages thirty-four to ninety-three for five years. The facilitators asked the participants two questions:

1. How much stress have you experienced in the last year?

2. How much time have you spent helping out neighbors, friends, and your community?

Then the facilitators used public records to find out who died.

What the study concluded was that people who experienced a big life stress had an increased risk of dying by 30%. However, people who who were active in their communities exhibited zero increased risk of stress-related death.

Sharing creates stress-resilience.

Human beings are designed to live in communities. When we share each other's burdens, the weight becomes much lighter. You share some of your burdens and take on some of others'. In this way, we are able to help each other move through really big stresses in life with virtually zero negative side effects.

If I didn't have Joanna and Justin in my life, I'm not sure what I would do when I have a problem or a question or a difficulty. They are the first two people I turn to when I need something, anything really.

If I hadn't made friends with the sisters on my team that year on N.E.T., I wouldn't have made it through that year. We were able to share the burdens and difficulties we had experienced in life up to that point and all of the other stresses that naturally came with working in ministry.

In the Gospel of Matthew, Jesus says, "Take my yoke upon you. Let me teach you... and you will find rest for your souls. For my yoke is easy to bear, and the burden I give you is light." (Matthew 11:29-30)

See, what happens is that Christ took our burdens to the cross and bore them in our place. He swapped our burdens for His own, so now the burden we bear is light and the one He bears is heavy. But He wants it this way. He wants to spread the load around so that not a single one of us is crushed by the weight.

Maybe you don't know who you should talk to or you're scared of what their reaction might be or you're not ready to share what's bothering you. Cast out a line and see what you catch. And remember this *very* important thing: many people won't know how to respond or how to help you. Don't let that reinforce any ideas that you are alone — you're not. You simply haven't found the right person for this time in your life. Don't stop trying. You will.

Sometimes the people that God has in mind for you are still being moved into place, and often they show up at the most unexpected times. Justin showed up in my life the moment I swore off boys. Joanna showed up in my life when I wasn't even in the same state.

If you're really not sure where to start, do something creative. Find a journal that speaks to you where you can start looking at your feelings take shape in front of you. Get some paint or colored pencils and just use the colors that mirror how to feel. Record a song. These mediums can help tremendously if you can't verbally share those things. Just let someone you trust read your journal, see your painting, hear your song, and then ask questions. Don't be afraid to answer honestly. Just open up a little to another human being.

Another reason creation is so powerful is because sometimes we just hurt and we don't know why. Using a creative medium can be a catalyst for self-discovery.

Additionally, try to find an adoration chapel near you. That is where Jesus is exposed in the form of the Eucharist for adorers to go and sit with him in the quiet. You will be shocked at how much love, clarity, and hope radiates from the Eucharist if you spend the time to soak it up. Open the Bible to whatever page comes to you and start reading. Recite any prayers you know by heart. Ask Jesus to start opening your heart so that you can recognize the truth and begin to heal.

Relationships Take Work

People are messy. Relationships take time and they take work.

I definitely have the mindset of an artist. I am an idealist and I am often selfish. People are not ideal, and they are often selfish themselves. That is what makes relationships hard and sometimes heartbreaking.

I very much did *not* want to take piano lessons when I was a child. I am still growing out of the very selfish notion that I should be able to do what I want when I want, and I wanted to learn piano *when* I wanted and *how* I wanted. I didn't want to be made to do it, to be told how to practice or what to play. Even at a very young age, I felt a strong creative independence and I didn't want to "sell out," as they say.

But in the fourth grade, Mom convinced me to start going to piano lessons. I *loved* playing! And I *hated* practicing. Mom would set an egg timer on the piano for twenty minutes and I had to practice those twenty minutes every day. She then caught on that I was only playing songs I had already learned and liked, and wasn't practicing the new songs I was supposed to be working on. So then she made sure I spent the twenty minutes practicing new things and then I could play the old pieces.

Without knowing it, I was learning discipline and also growing in creativity. It definitely wasn't fun all the time, but I fell in love with the process and that made the hard time worth it.

The mindset of an artist will tell you that rules and "work" kill creativity. I have often felt that way, but experience has taught me otherwise. Rules and restrictions increase your potential for creativity. Just watch an episode of *Chopped*! Learning where the lines are allows you to decide when and how to cross them. Necessity is the mother of invention, and when your routine is shaken or your normal materials are altered, something new can be created.

When I started sharing my songs with other people and hearing their reactions and opinions, I felt unsafe. I worried that people would find out I was actually a terrible musician. Plus, my shrouded and buried feelings were being dug up and that was uncomfortable, yet important.

Because I have now been through the process of sharing so many times, I have no problem sharing my work with others and accepting their critiques. I very often share my deep (and often odd) questions with

Justin and Joanna and I can take their feedback from a detached place that allows me to assess it.

It is through sharing in relationships that we begin to heal and better understand ourselves, and you have to do it over and over again for it to get easier.

Discussion Questions

Self-Esteem

After reading this book and reflecting on these questions, rate yours self-esteem from 1-10 once again. _____

Communication

1. Who is someone in your life that you unquestioningly trust?

2. What is one thing you know you have difficulty sharing?

3. Is there a creative medium that you can use or are already using to express your emotions?

Love Languages

1. What do you think your primary love language is?

2. How can you better love others by identifying their love language?

3. Think of a time that you felt unloved. What do you think made you feel that way?

Loneliness

1. Think of a time that you felt alone. What do you think made you feel that way? Is there something you could have done or someone you could have sought out to reconnect?

2. What communities are you a part of? What communities would you like to connect with?

Relationships

1. What is the messiest relationship that you have? Why?

2. What is the most fulfilling and helpful relationship that you have? Why?

Action Item

Choose one thing that you can DO in the next month to begin changing something you are currently unhappy with. Write it down and refer to it often.

Part 4. Epilogue

In the seven years since I served with N.E.T. Ministries, I have used my gifts of writing and music to serve many people and communities. I have slowly grown in self-awareness and continue to grow through journaling and writing music.

I have been (mostly) healed of those detrimental paradigms I set for myself in my adolescence by turning my gaze towards my purpose in life and deriving all truth and worth from God.

I have continued to use my gift of music to celebrate weddings, ceremoniously say goodbye to deceased loved ones at their funerals, praise and worship the Lord with many charismatic prayer groups, and supply music for the Catholic Mass.

I never thought I would have the confidence, the self-esteem, or the knowledge that could get to me to this place in life. I am peaceful, whole, and undoubtedly loved. I want that for you.

I hope that my story has either solidified those same things in your own life or has catapulted you on a journey to discovering them.

I would love to know your story. If you would like to share it or have any questions or comments, please visit my website at www.emilyfaithe.com or send me a direct email at emily@emilyfaithe.com.

Part 5. Exercises

Letter Exercise

Write a letter to someone that you feel you can't express yourself to. Deliver it to them in whatever way possible.

Journal Exercise

If you don't already, begin keeping a journal. Keep track of how you are feeling day to day, the things that bring you joy, and the aspirations you have for your life. Every month, go back and recap what you've written and make a plan to improve anything you are unhappy with.

About The Author

EMILY FAITHE currently lives in Pembroke, NH with her husband Justin. She grew up in Salem, NH with her parents, two sisters, and brother. She received a Bachelor's Degree in Music Education from the University of New Hampshire and is now using all that she has learned and experienced to help others tell their stories and transform into healthy, whole, faithful people.

Learn more about Emily at emilyfaithe.com.

You can also check out Emily's blogging project, where she is helping Catholics everywhere grow in their faith www.catholicparishsupport.com.

One Last Thing...

If you enjoyed this book or found it useful, I'd be very grateful if you'd post a **short review on Amazon**. Your words really do make a difference and I read all the reviews personally so I can get your feedback and make this book even better.

More importantly, if you have friends or family that need to read this book, PLEASE tell them about it.

I would also *love* to hear your stories of trial and triumph,

so please visit my author page: emilyfaithe.com/musicsavedmylife

or the Facebook Fan Page: https://www.facebook.com/emilypetersonfreelancewriter

and leave me a note!

Thanks again for your support!

Notes

_____

_____

_____

_____

_____

_____

_____

_____

_____

_____

Notes

_____

_____

_____

_____

_____

_____

_____

_____

_____

_____

Notes

Notes

_____

_____

_____

_____

_____

_____

_____

_____

_____

_____

Notes

_____

_____

_____

_____

_____

_____

_____

_____

_____

Notes

_____

_____

_____

_____

_____

_____

_____

_____

_____

_____